CODED FOR MONEY, FLOW AND FAME

THE DIFFERENCE BETWEEN YOU CHASING CLIENTS AND THEM CHASING YOU

SARAH QUINN

Red Thread Publishing LLC. 2021

Write to info@redthreadbooks.com if you are interested in publishing with Red Thread Publishing. Learn more about publications or foreign rights acquisitions of our catalog of books: www.redthreadbooks.com

Paperback ISBN : **978-1-955683-10-4**

To the two humans who make creating a legacy entirely worth it. You are my whole world. Every person this book impacts will be in thanks to you.

CONTENTS

Introduction   1

WHAT NOT TO DO SO YOU CAN BECOME
AN EXPERT AT AUTHORITY MARKETING

Break The Rules. Break All The Fucking Rules.   7

Assignment One   11

Credibility Won't Come From Viewers   12
Watching Your Dog Learn To Sit

Assignment Two   15

Quoting Other Experts Sells THEM, Not You   16

Assignment Three   19

You Can Do Anything But You Cannot Do   20
Everything

Assignment Four   23

The Very Public Break Up   24

Assignment Five   27

YOU'VE GOT THE GOODS, LET'S GET IT
OUT TO THE WORLD

Authority Marketing Statement   31

Assignment Six   35

Tell Great Stories All Day Long!   36

Assignment Seven   41

It's Time to Raise Your Hands Ladies and   43
Gents

Assignment Eight   47

Questions That Quantum Leap Success   48

Assignment Nine   51

Where You May Get Stuck   53

Client Success Story   55

A SNEAK PEEK INSIDE HAVE IT ALL - STEP
UP, LET SUCCESS FLOW. 30-DAY MONEY
MINDSET FOR COACHES

Book #1 Quit Fucking Around Series   59

A SNEAK PEEK INSIDE 100-DAY JOURNAL
PROMPTS FOR READY TO BE 6 & 7 FIGURE
COACHES

Book #2 Quit Fucking Around Series   67

About the Author   71
Other Books by Sarah Quinn   73
So What Now?   75
About Red Thread Publishing   77
Leave a Review   79

INTRODUCTION

I don't know about you, but when I hear the word authority, I do this quick lip jerk on the left side, while my eyes instantly widen. I can think of a dozen times in my adult life where I broke the rules (judge me if you must), but those were some of the best moments I've ever had. I was born to be a rule-breaker, so naturally, I went against my norm, and became an expert at authority marketing. Go figure. The thing I'd been defying my whole life became my profession and my passion.

If this is your first Sarah Quinn read, let me tell you, you picked a good one. The Quit Fucking Around Series was written to help coaches, consultants and entrepreneurs cover every basis possible needed to have BOTH success AND fulfilment.

Book #1 - *Have It All* covers the most important piece, your money mindset. I can teach you everything there is to know about marketing, but if you repel money or lose it as fast as you get it because of what feels like very real fear, you're still going to be stuck.

Book #2 - *100-Day Journal Prompts* covers alignment, wealth, strategy, and creating the only kind of success that matters, the kind YOU choose.

And finally, *Coded For Money, Flow and Fame*, it's here to teach you HOW to create wealth, experience flow, and be seen as the expert you are.

You're about to dive into the no-bullshit zone. This is a "say it like you need to hear it, absorb it as if your life depends on it, and act like it matters to take action now" kind of book. It factors in zero touchy-feely, hand-holding, whatever you currently feel about marketing, specifically your marketing. It doesn't matter.

I'm not trying to be insensitive. I want to help you get results. Like 24-hour turnaround results. At the end of each chapter, I'm going to give you an assignment. Those of you who use them will see results; those of you who don't, won't. Plain and simple.

What if I told you that marketing isn't about your program, product, or service at all? If you're anything like my clients (and since you're reading this, I presume you are), you've tried at least one coach, maybe even two or three. You've bought at least one $27 batch of prettied-up social media post templates from some guru—who, by the way, is sadly not a guru at marketing; they are—however, a guru at pretty templates. But I imagine you didn't really want pretty templates. You wanted to make social media easier or less time-consuming, and so the 'ONLY $27' templates seemed like the perfect option. You then realized that pretty templates aren't going to sell for you. That sucks. I totally feel for you, but the reality is that entrepreneurs make these mistakes every single day, sometimes over and over.

You've either hired someone on Fiverr, a social media person, a VA, or maybe all of the above, to help you with your marketing, since we're here on this very page together right now. My guess is the results you wanted either didn't happen, or they didn't last.

I want you to pause reading right now and remind yourself out loud, so you can hear it in your own voice, that you are so damn incredible, and so clearly committed, that even though X, Y and Z didn't work, you haven't given up on your dreams. You see, trying and failing is the true definition of winning (let's all quote this one on Facebook because it's totally worthy of that.) And here's what I want you to take away from this: you picking up this book to try and gain insight into how to market, AKA get more clients, even with all the wasted time and money, proves you have what it takes to succeed, and you should own that because you totally deserve it.

I've met 1000s of entrepreneurs who have tried dozens of strategies, and most of them just threw their hands in the air and said, 'Well, that didn't work,' and they stayed stuck. No sales, just resentment, guilt, and a sense of failure because they couldn't "make business work." But not you! Because you've landed here in this book, where the following pages are full of the tools any coach, entrepreneur, or sales rep can use in any industry to get noticed, create leads, and close sales.

You want to make money, right? You want to help more people, right? Here's how you do it...

i LOVED this morning. What is your mothly cost to be with you? I love directness and I need help. I've got the value, I want help so that I can make money by supporting others to remove the pain that I'm feeling in my business now.

you are sweet I'm so glad you got the benefit.

I'd suggest as a starter the mastermind because it focuses on foundation AND sales

This client listened to a 15-minute class I taught and had NEVER had a conversation with me about my program. Within 15 minutes of her sending this message she was signed up and onboarded. No selling necessary.

WHAT NOT TO DO SO YOU CAN BECOME AN EXPERT AT AUTHORITY MARKETING

BREAK THE RULES. BREAK ALL THE FUCKING RULES.

Break the rules. Break all the fucking rules.

Because what you've been taught about marketing is that there is a #1 strategy you can use to boost your Instagram followers. How did that work for you?

Or that you can insert ___, swipe, copy, and close more deals from your email campaigns? Close any deals lately?

When it comes to marketing, some things are meant to work well for some people, some for some industries, and some for some kinds of promotions. But authority works. Every. Damn. Time. When we apply it to marketing, it works for everyone. Always, in every niche, 100% of the time.

So what is authority marketing? Explained simply, it's the elevation of an expert to a standard, so great that people just know they want to consume whatever this person puts out, often without questioning it. That last part is key, and your golden ticket to successfully market your book, so let me repeat it for those in the back: *often without questioning it.*

What exactly do I mean? I mean that you can elevate yourself to a standard so high that you no longer have to "sell."

The most common thing I hear from clients is "Sarah, I hate selling!" I can honestly say that I don't feel like I've ever sold a person a single day in my life, and I close deals daily. I don't want you to have to ask people to buy from you. I want you to be able to just share your badass content so that people say, "Hey! How do I buy your X," and then all you have to do is give them the link, or perhaps share some basic details they may be needing.

Maybe I should have been a little more direct earlier on. Break the rules, break all the fucking rules, specifically ALL the ones that you are already using that clearly aren't working.

No BS here. There are a ton of things you are doing that just aren't working. Let's take podcasting, for example. How many of you are thrilled when you get asked to be a guest speaker on a podcast? I'll bet all of you. But how many of you have ever gotten a client from it? From experience, I could say probably very few of you, if any of you. And the reason for that is, what you've been taught is that you get an offer for a podcast recording, you create a Facebook post saying that you are going to be a guest speaker on such and such podcast, you do the episode, maybe the day of you create a second post saying, "recording podcast with so and so today." And when the podcast goes live, you go on your Facebook page, your LinkedIn and your Instagram and you share the link for the recording. And then you get on with your day.

How's this working for you? We want to toss this strategy, like, yesterday, because *I want you to get results.* I want you to be seen as an expert. I want you to get on a podcast, and convert listeners into leads and leads into sales because that's what you were meant to do; you were meant to be out there, impacting people, making a difference, and making a bucket load of money doing it. So at the end of this chapter, I'm going to give you a strategy on how to set yourself up for success when podcasting. But let's get back to it, because there are other things that you are currently doing that are a waste of time and are harming your position in the marketplace.

I know that what you want is to help people, so let's start by taking a good look at what NOT to do with your marketing. I want you to stop doing this now. Today. In fact, go back over your last seven days of posts on social media and remove anything that represents the below strategies you've currently been using to fill your feed. I'd rather you have a blank feed than one that hurts your position in the marketplace.

ASSIGNMENT ONE

- Get honest with yourself right here, right now. What is your current position in the marketplace? Does your audience REALLY know what you do? Is your audience 500 people or 50,000 people? Would you say you are in front of the right people or that you are still working on that?How are sales going? Do you feel like you are excited to share your offer or are you uncomfortable with this?
- Knowing where you stand is the first step to understanding why sales may not be coming in. I've provided a few lines here for you to jot down your findings.

CREDIBILITY WON'T COME FROM VIEWERS WATCHING YOUR DOG LEARN TO SIT

First, there should be no sharing daily photos of your pet, the food you ate today, and especially unbearably perplexing things that you saw in a Walmart parking lot. This elevates you in no way, shape, or form as an expert. It means your audience is consuming useless information from you. And what good does that really do you, or them? Worse still, it means your attention when you show up is on the wrong things. Unless you can tell your audience how the new trick your dog learned solves their problem, it's not helpful.

I get it. You want to spend time sharing with people how authentic you are. But again, we want to keep people focused on what really matters about your business. Sure, your cuddly pet is cute, but your social feed has the potential to be about so much more. Think of it this way, your social feed is about your ability to impact and change the life of another human being for the better. So let's show up with things that impact that!

. . .

Note: Do share your incredible life milestones as, of course, this keeps you human and relatable.

Here's a great example:

Celebrating our new dog Rufus. I always thought I was too busy to take care of a pet. I felt like every waking moment had to be about my business. EVERYONE MEET RUFUS! He's now part of the family all thanks to me doing the exact same work I teach my clients: How Not To Let Your Business Rule Your Life.

(insert cute dog photo here)

See how I tie this life event into my marketing strategy? This supports my overall message AND shows people I'm a human living the life I want while still crushing it in my business.

ASSIGNMENT TWO

- Pick a recent life milestone and practice crafting a message while tying it back into your marketing. Tip: Feel free to check the bio section of the book for my Facebook community. You can paste in your milestone message and I'll personally give you some feedback.

QUOTING OTHER EXPERTS
SELLS THEM, NOT YOU

L et's take a look at the latest trend of inspirational quotes, shall we? Quotes from experts you've never met, been mentored by, or have never actually connected with, have zero business being on your feed. Let them be on everyone else's. Unless, of course, you think somehow raising other experts magically makes you more appealing as an expert. Has anyone ever bought your product because you can quote Winston Churchill? No offence, Winston, and I say this with great love and respect, but here's how this is playing out. You have an ever-so-important task to do that for whatever reason you keep putting off (it's probably a task that will actually make you more or create more ease). And instead of facing it, you aimlessly scroll Instagram or Pinterest, or perhaps your Face-book feed, and there it is! Someone has posted a quote by their favorite mentor or author, and you think to yourself, oh my god, that's so true. I think people should do this/think this/feel this/be this. You quickly download the image to your phone, hop over to your own feed, and share it. You write this off as a truly productive day because you got something posted on social media and you promised yourself you'd do this today.

Why. Do. You. Do. This?

Did you act on the valuable lesson from that quote or did you post it and just keep on scrolling? Chances are, like most people, you kept scrolling.

People are going to do the exact same thing when they see the quote on your wall. They're going to copy, paste, and share.

So, who or how does this help? Well, for starters, the quote becomes memorable and of course the names of the person who said it does, too. And if you are lucky, the rare person will come along, make this their life mantra, do the work and live a crazy amazing life, but most people will just copy, paste, and share.

But what if the quote on your wall was yours? What if you took the brilliant stuff that flies out of your mouth and shared that? And then someone else shared that? And someone else, and so on, and then you become the famous person? Everyone keeps sharing, and it's your name up there for everyone to read and recognize. What would that do for you and your image vs. you sharing someone else's name?

By sharing your own words, you become an expert.

Now let's take a look at the other side of posting quotes. Quoting things your clients' contacts and community say about you, your program, and your service. This is a major authority marketing YES! In fact, it's a resounding yes. It feels like bragging because it is. And Babycakes, it's okay.

Please remember, we're here to break the rules. You're out there helping people and you're bragging because you are damn good at it. Think of it this way: the more you brag, the more people you get to help.

ASSIGNMENT THREE

- Go back through any Facebook lives, sales call recordings, blogs, anything and everything you have, and create a list of 6 quotes you can share on your social media.

YOU CAN DO ANYTHING BUT YOU CANNOT DO EVERYTHING

Y ou Can Do Anything, but you cannot do everything. Well, you can. But not well.

Some of you are so busy trying to show the world you're freakin' fantastic by being involved in nine different business ventures. That's not crazy, but the way you are building it is!

Think about it this way. If you were going to give me your money to solve a problem, you'd likely want to know a few things, such as:

I truly understand your problem.

I've solved this problem before.

I have the time and energy to dedicate to you.

So when you are showcasing the 9 different business ventures you are involved in (that probably have nothing to do with one another), are you helping or harming your marketing?

I am all about multiple streams of income. In fact, I praise those who can achieve this. But you're confusing the shit out of your audience when you ask them to buy your course, laugh about your cat, get in a debate about what you saw in the Walmart parking lot, pick their favorite essential oil (that, of course, is on sale so they NEED to buy it today), AND sign up to distribute cleaning products.

Do you see where I am going with this? Become an expert at *one thing*; become so well known for it that everyone is REALLY clear about who you are, who you help, how you help them, and what results they will get. Once you are established as an expert, you can THEN step into sharing your other talents... one at a time.

If your social feed resembles even half of the list above, my head is spinning for you. It's clear this is why people aren't buying from you... you are that gal or guy who everyone is trying to avoid because "Oh great, what are they into now?"

You don't want to be that person, do you? Stop that shit and get clear, my love.

ASSIGNMENT FOUR

- How will you know when your audience
  understands what your business is really about?
  What kinds of things will happen? What kinds of
  things will they say to you? If this isn't already
  happening, what will you do to ensure extreme
  clarity for your audience?

THE VERY PUBLIC BREAK UP

As in, public debates where sellers break up their audience.

The goal with authority marketing is to bring TOGETHER like-minded prospects (we'll get into this more later when we get into philosophical marketing).

When you post debatable content, you basically become the referee between a now very divided community.

I want to flick people in the forehead when I see this because it's one of the worst things you can do. You may as well post: "Hey Joe, meet Samantha here in my network. She is 100% for vaccines and you are 100% against them... please buy my course."

Joe and Samantha are too busy foaming at the mouth while they battle out who's right and who's wrong about vaccines (hopefully in a private chat, but let's be real, this very public debate is likely happening right on your Facebook wall for everyone to see and engage with).

"But I am so passionate about X, Sarah!"

GREAT! I'm passionate about the way the hot married guy down the hall looks, but I don't jump his bones just because I'm passionate.

"I'm about to start WW3 with wifey if I do this, and then how am I going to feel every time I walk out my condo door?"

Some of you have taken what authenticity is supposed to be and turned it into the #1 reason you have ZERO clients. And yes, I understand what freedom of speech is, and Luv, you can speak freely. But beware, there are consequences, and your sales are right up there in the top 3 things this is impacting.

Unless your job is to sell people on the fact that they should/shouldn't get vaccinated, do you really NEED to post your opinion on this?

By removing these four things from your social feeds, AND social conversations, you leave room for what really matters to your audience: education, connection, and conversation.

ASSIGNMENT FIVE

- Your assignment here is to get clear on what it is you ARE selling people on. Please remember, nobody wakes up in the morning thinking, OMG, I want a new membership today. They wake up thinking:

> I can't stand...
> I'm so tired of...
> UGH, if only we could...
> I'm so sick and tired of...
> I can't take another day of...
> If I have to ___ one more time I'm going to___

- Fill these in for your perfect client. And in the space provided, get clear on the transformation you are selling because really, THAT is what they are buying.

YOU'VE GOT THE GOODS, LET'S GET IT OUT TO THE WORLD

Knowing what not to do is super important, but I have to be honest, I am more excited that we are going to dive in now on what TO DO to be seen as an expert in the marketplace.

We're going to dive into the 4 pillars of successful authority marketing.

1. A successful authority marketing statement
2. Stories of transformation
3. The raising of the hands posts
4. Asking the right questions

Let's take a deeper look, shall we?

AUTHORITY MARKETING
STATEMENT

Your authority marketing statement is a statement that gives you, your audience, and your leads clarity. Its simplicity may fool you into thinking it's not important, but I promise you, it's essential.

I am___(title). I help___(your perfect client), so that___(the transformation they want) by___(what is the process you use to achieve this).

It's one simple phrase not meant to be too wordy or complicated and designed to get straight to the point.

I AM ____

Now some of you will try to come up with some fancy pants title for yourself.

DON'T!

I once had a client who helped women leave their corporate careers to become successful entrepreneurs, and in her authority marketing statement she wrote, 'I am a career change agent.'

Can anyone tell me what a career change agent is?

Blinking rapidly over there? My guess is you can't because it's not a real thing. When you come up with these so-called branded titles, you confuse your audience. Yes, there is something unique in having a signature statement, and we will get to this.

If a doctor suddenly called themselves a trained medical support leader, you'd skip over that in the yellow pages and search for DOCTOR.

I HELP ___

Some of you will try to help everyone with a statement like, "I'm a money mindset coach. I help moms so that they can have more money by..."

But what kind of moms? Young moms? Old moms? Single moms? Struggling moms? Entrepreneurial moms?

Again. Get specific.

SO THAT ___

When you get into the "so that" section, keep it to the over-arching thing you do. This is not the place to list the 100 benefits they have, but rather to help them address their REAL problem.

Someone looking for leads doesn't really want leads; they want sales.

So let's frame this. I am a business coach. I help brand new entrepreneurs so that they can get sales quickly by...

BY ___

And lastly, the 'by' section. How you help people doesn't matter as much as the fact that you do actually help people, BUT, everyone wants to know the answer to the magic question: HOW. So let's create some clarity while amplifying their confidence in you.

The 'by' section can be a bit tricky, so let me share an example with you.

If your name is Frank Mendez and you are an investment coach who takes a 6-step approach to help people get started with investing, you'd put something like the Mendez 6-Step Method to Investing.

So let's run through a full Authority Marketing Statement so you can see what it should look like:

I am an authority marketing expert. I help coaches, consultants, and entrepreneurs so that they can become the top 5% of performers in their industry by positioning them as experts with my authority accelerator formula.

This statement does 3 core things:

- It gets you clear on what you do and who your audience is.
- It helps your readers to be able to see instantly if you have what they are looking for.
- It tells people without them having to ask what results they can expect from you, and how they will get them.

ASSIGNMENT SIX

WHO YOU ARE	WHO YOUR CLIENT IS
I AM	I HELP

YOUR RESULTS	YOUR OFFER
SO THAT	BY

TELL GREAT STORIES ALL DAY LONG!

Tell great stories all day long. It's that simple. If you want to sell, just keep telling great stories.

I don't mean any story. I mean authority marketing stories—the kind that sells people on how amazing you are and teaches them why they should buy from you.

...and how do I do THAT, Sarah?

You use the Quinn Success Story Method.

We're going to use storytelling to create social proof, letting your audience have a taste of what it's like to work with you.

Most coaches give the who, what, and why when they tell stories. But not you, because you are an expert. You are going to give the who, what, when, where, why, AND how.

To make this really easy, we're going to break it down into 4 simple sections.

Where I was. + What I did. + Where I am. + Why You Need to Know.

WHERE I WAS: Includes the who, the when, and the what.

. . .

WHAT I DID: Includes the what and the how.

WHERE I AM: Includes the where (where you are in life/business because of the 'WHAT I DID').

WHY YOU NEED TO KNOW: Includes the why and the how (how your audience takes the next steps).

The reason why this is so dang powerful is because everyone wants to understand HOW the transformation will happen, and they want proof you've done this before with real-live people. This is also REALLY powerful because the perfect client will read this and go, "DANG! That sounds like me, I need to try that too!" Here is where you tap into their feelings on such a deep level that you force them to look internally. And for most people, when they take a look at what's happening inside, they recognize it's time to make a change.

I want to cover all of my bases here because I have heard clients say it OVER and OVER... "I can't do these kinds of posts, Sarah, because of privacy issues." I call BS, and here's why. It takes a split second to change a name or drop the line "name changed to protect client privacy" at the bottom of a post.

No excuses Luv, we're here to make an impact, no matter what it takes.

Let's play this out in short form, and know you can always elaborate a bit more on these.

Laura was desperate to escape her toxic relationship. After buying my new book, How to Leave Toxic Relationships In 10 Steps, she learned that truly loving herself means self-respect at the deepest core level, and putting up with someone who always made her feel down wasn't self-respect. Now, Laura has left her relationship in only 2 weeks from the day she picked up my book. Why am I telling you this? Because my readers have major transformations, and if you're like Laura, stuck in an unhappy relationship, wondering if this is it for you or feeling like there is no way out, or even if you've been sitting around for the last 5 years wanting to be a wife with no ring on your finger while the resentment builds inside of you, this book is for you.

Do a Laura-style life shift and start with grabbing your copy of How to Leave Toxic Relationships here -> (insert link)

These kinds of stories are bold social proof that your book can give the reader their desired outcome. It will also help the right person to buy, meaning you will have a tribe of loyal followers who are more than excited to share your book with their gal pals in the same situation.

How to have clients come to you because YOU are the expert.

You know when you see people post on social media, "what book are you reading?" This is where they insert your name excitedly.

Let me share another example with you. This one shows one of my client's posts and then shows how it is re-written with the depth of authority marketing.

Client Version:

L. came to me after a particularly messy break-up she had relocated for. She felt lost & overwhelmed. Like so many of my clients, L knew something needed to happen but didn't know where to start. I guided her through my fulfillment formula and with the tools she learned, L was able to—unpack all that had happened—grieve what she had lost—AND reconnect with herself to find the answers she was seeking! With the surety/clarity she gained from the process, she was able to flourish: 1. Within 2 months she moved to her dream city, and 2. Started a business that fused her passions. Now, almost two years later, she is still using the tools I taught her to navigate the inevitable challenges life throws. If you are ready for results like these, it is time for you to go on the same journey as L to craft YOUR meaningful & Fulfilled life!

Rewrite:

Break-ups break you up, sometimes a little, sometimes a lot... and sometimes, the more of them you have, the more they break you all over.

Suzanna and I met inside a mutual online social group. She had started following my newsfeed to gain inspiration about life and fulfillment.

She had recently gone through a messy break-up. You know, the one that makes you feel so bad you want to escape your own skin, and since you can't, you escape town.

The damage a relationship can do can be so harmful you literally just feel better in an entirely new location.

As you can imagine, Suzanna was feeling completely lost and broken inside. I remember the day she first connected with me; she was searching for something to take the pain away. Someone to understand what she was going through.

It wasn't long before she realized that she needed to make some major changes in her life to feel whole again.

We dove deep into my Fulfillment Formula used to guide men and women from feeling stuck into creating a process that allows them to feel fueled with the possibility of taking action and moving forward.

In 3 short months, Suzanna was able to:

- *Truly unpack all that had happened in the relationship, owning both her side of the journey and accepting what had happened on his.*
- *Have a safe place where she felt seen, heard, and understood, to grieve what she had lost.*
- *Reconnect with her truest desires and start taking steps to build a more fulfilling life than the one she had been living before.*

It can be hard to reach out for support when you are feeling down, but courage is the starting point of possibility, and Suzanna used her courage to show up for herself.

Within 2 months of working together, she not only began to heal from the relationship, but she was also able to move to her dream city loving the skin she was in and begin building a business that truly fueled her inner passions. Almost two years later, she is still using the tools she learned during the Fulfillment Formula program to navigate the inevitable challenges life throws.

I may not be a relationship expert, but what I can tell you is, relationship or not, if you are ready for results like these in any area of your life, it is time for you to go on the same journey as Suzanna and craft YOUR meaningful & Fulfilled life!

P.S. The name of this story has been changed to protect the privacy of this honored client.

ASSIGNMENT SEVEN

- In order to write good stories, you must understand your clients' pains and desires. Use the following worksheet to get clear on what your client is experiencing and what they really want.

Pains   Desires

IT'S TIME TO RAISE YOUR HANDS LADIES AND GENTS

There is something I like to call the raising of the hands posts. They are by far the easiest way to identify who your next clients will be. They have 2 purposes:

- To pre-qualify prospects
- To create social awareness of how friggin' amazing you are

Let's take a look at the first set of posts, what I call the "pre-qual" posts.

Prequalifying, in simple terms, is your awareness that a prospect is an excellent fit for your product and that they meet the necessary requirements to gain success from investing in you. What you want to have is an audience raising their hand and saying, "Hey Sarah, over here!! Notice me? That solution you keep bragging about, I have a problem to match it!"

And now you position your XYZ offer in front of them and voila, a sale is born.

Some quick examples:

You all know by now I write romance novels. Raise your hand if you're looking for a new read for your next vacay.

Anyone who chimes in saying "ME!" is going to get one of these messages in return: "OMG, where are you headed on vacation? My readers have been bragging about how my new book, Sally Meets Martin, is the most romantic vacation read ever! I'd love to know if you feel the same. You can grab your copy to take with you, and p.s. Amazon ships in like 2 days, so you'll get it quick -> (insert link to book here)"

These posts are what I like to call catching the low-hanging fruit and hell yes, it's fruitful!

The second style is designed to create social awareness of how friggin' amazing you and your book are.

Here is an example:

Here's why this works. There are three levels of influence where a buyer buys. External, internal, and philosophical.

External is when a buyer basically impulse buys. "I want a book- the cover of it looks cool. I'm gonna buy it." This is the rarest buy and often the least satisfied buy.

Most sales social posts are done in a way to attract impulse buyers because it's just link posting instead of content creation, and if you notice I said this is the rarest buy, you can see what you are doing wrong.

Internal is when a buyer buys based on a feeling and a belief. It's backed by internal understanding. "I feel so lonely but when I pick up a romance novel I get lost in the love story and it gives me so much hope."

This is an easy sell because we support a current emotional belief, so they are already attracted to what we have to offer.

Philosophical is when a group of people with strong common beliefs are together in one space. Because their common belief is so strong, when one says "yes", they almost all say "yes."

For example: If there is a tour put on for animal activists and they are touring a rainforest, let's say one of the attendees sees an injured bird with its beak stuck in a water bottle (stay with me here). If one of the activists says "This is outrageous, we should protest the pollution around here!" The likelihood is, the others will follow suit and be on board.

The same is true for selling. This is why it's crucial to fill your social channels with those who are like-minded, and then create a stream of "raising my hand to celebrate Jane Doe for enrolling in my free masterclass - How to Have a Happy Marriage."

OR

"Lifting my hands to celebrate a new book sale."

OR

"OMG, this just in - 3 new buyers are going to learn how to XYZ - celebrate with me."

Note: If you take each one of these wins and turn it into a story post after, your social feed will become a goldmine.

ASSIGNMENT EIGHT

- I've put together an easy-to-follow course with over 100 fill-in-the-blank social media posts that you can use to get your audience to raise their hands and say "Hey, me, over here, I'm your client!"

I've opened up the course ONLY for those who have purchased Coded For Money, Flow and Fame for only $20. You can click here https://www.sarahquinncoaching.com/offers/XLrogXDq to access the course and start taking BIG action today.

QUESTIONS THAT QUANTUM LEAP SUCCESS

And lastly, asking the right questions.

Knowing what to say to your audience can be the hardest part of marketing because up until now you've probably been bombarded with courses and programs that teach you how to "create the perfect IG post" or "buy these 24 Canva templates and rock your marketing." Let me guess, it's not working! *What does work?* you're probably wondering.

Well, I will be the first to tell you to save your money; you don't need those. AT. ALL.

I believe you can HAVE IT ALL on your terms, exactly as you wish; so if what you want is to post once a day and have major success, then ask the right questions.

How can I achieve posting as little as possible but still have a mountain of traction around my book?

Everyone's answer will vary, but you could come up with something like "I'll have ambassadors who post about me so I don't have to post as often." Or, "I'll speak at events and sell my books there."

Maybe you are the opposite and love the energy that

comes from a fully engaged social community, so posting often is what fuels you.

The question you'd want to ask yourself is, "How do I show up often without burning out?"

Here you may discover that to be a rockstar at social media you don't have to create 20 NEW posts a week. You can create 5 and rework them into multiple posts.

Asking the right questions isn't just key in how you become a successful authority marketer; it's how you become fulfilled and successful in life.

You may notice that I didn't mention anything about setting goals for your marketing. I didn't ask you to pick a number of clients you want to have, because honestly, if you sold to 1000 people and it was easy, would it be enough? What about 10,000 people, if it were easy; would that be enough?

No, because if it were easy, you'd sell all day, every day. You'd impact more people, and make more money. Rather than setting a target, I want you to set a standard.

ASSIGNMENT NINE

I want you to pick a goal. Let it be anything you could ever possibly imagine for your business.

In the space provided, I want you to start asking yourself questions. And yes, I want you to answer yourself! They could look like:

- Who can get me in front of 500+ of my target audience?
- What belief do I need to let go of to achieve X?
- If I increased my price from X to Y, what # of sales would I only have to hit to achieve my sales goal?

These are just some examples of really great questions.

This is the kind of stuff others can really learn from, so please take a photo of this and share it in the Facebook group so others can learn some amazing questions to kick start their success.

https://www.facebook.com/
groups/codedformoneyflowandfame

Be sure to #codedformoneyflowandfame so I can give you a personal shout-out!

WHERE YOU MAY GET STUCK

I've worked with entrepreneurs for over 14 years now, and sadly, I still get asked the same questions today as I did years ago. That tells me the information out there on the internet is more harmful than helpful, and that's probably because there is so darn much of it.

I get it. You are overloaded with information. So what is right and what is wrong?

The honest answer: Nothing is right or wrong, it's about what works for you. Authority marketing is designed to work in every industry, niche, and for every phase of a marketing plan.

It gets people informed AND gets them to tell you if they need your help so you aren't out there chasing your tail around trying to figure out who may or may not be your client.

So when people ask me things like *"how many times a day should I post?"* My answer is, I don't know, I don't care, just do what works for you and your audience.

If you love posting 10 times a day, and you post relevant content, then post 10 times a day.

If you hate posting and post once a week, post once a week.

If you post once a week and hate getting little to no sales because you lack visibility and connection, hire someone to do it for you and let them decide what's needed.

There is no magic formula. I know, you probably paid a lot of money for someone to tell you there was, once upon a time.

You are in the driver's seat here. Build a business that you love, and others will love it too. It's really that simple.

If your next question is *"But Sarah, should I have a podcast?"*

Well, yes or no. You decide. If a podcast excites you and you want to show up for it, then do that.

If having a podcast means more work and you aren't really going to do it, or worse, you are going to do it but you aren't going to monetize it, then maybe it's not a great fit for you.

I'm sure this isn't what you thought I would add to the end of the book. But the truth is, so many of you THINK marketing is hard, and IT IS, but only because **you are making it hard**.

My rule of thumb is always to ask myself: *"If I do X, is it helping or harming my sales?"*

If the answer is yes, I do it. If the answer is I don't know, I try it. If the answer is no, I don't waste my time. If the answer is *I don't know, let me try it*, and then it bores me or doesn't produce results, or takes more time than it's worth, I stop. Let your marketing be fun. Let it be about you and your audience. After all, you are the one who has to show up for it for the rest of your business' life. Shouldn't you at least enjoy it a little?

I**t only took 2 weeks of her shifting her messaging to bring on a new client.**
Authority marketing IS the game-changer that WILL close you more clients, attract serious leads and be the reason your revenue grows this year.

Aleasha had been following me on social media for a few months and was working to shift her marketing message. She found that no matter how many times she shifted her authority marketing statement she was still not getting the traction she wanted. Aleasha enrolled in It's Time For 6 Mastermind where I teach coaches and entrepreneurs how to hit the 6 figure mark and in just two and a half weeks of transitioning her messaging based on her clients pains and desires and structuring her content to help people see her as the expert she is, she landed a new high ticket client.

Let's look at what she did to make this shift:

- She got clear on who she was, who she served, how she serves them, and what their results are.
- She stopped talking about the # of hours of coaching

people would get and the # of videos in her program, and talked about pains and desires.

- *She knew her audience inside and out, remembering that she is her best client.*

Most importantly, she knows that being the go-to person in her industry means closing sales is almost effortless.

A SNEAK PEEK INSIDE HAVE IT ALL - STEP UP, LET SUCCESS FLOW. 30-DAY MONEY MINDSET FOR COACHES

Get Your Copy Here

You get to be wealthy because you decide you deserve it.

Sunday afternoons have always been about one thing, dreaming about how wealthy people lived. I would walk through houses that started in the low millions and drive cars that had more fancy tech than the electronic store. I certainly couldn't afford any of it then, but I damn sure knew I loved being around it. I'm sure one can agree that it was wrong to waste the realtor's time pretending I could afford a home I'd later go home and dream of having, but this was my first taste into what money could buy and I loved it, especially the stainless steel in the kitchen, the 20+

acres of beautiful land, and the smell of the leather seats in the shiny new car.

I wanted to experience this every day.

So, for the next 10 very long years, I worked 12-14 hour days and guess what, I got nowhere fast.

Sure, I made money, but it always seemed to go out as fast as it came in. I worked harder and longer, and then, I hit burnout. Maybe you've been there, and if you haven't let me tell you, true burn out leaves you feeling paralyzed and so exhausted you can't do a thing. At this point, I had dropped all the fancy balls I was juggling in the air and wasn't even able to balance my work.

Money took on a whole new face then. Forget the car and the mansion. How the hell was I going to pay my bills? Feed my kids? Cover car insurance? I didn't have enough to get by, let alone keep dreaming big.

And that was that. All of my dreams vanished along with my belief I could have it all.

I couldn't figure out what I did wrong. I mean, I worked my friggin' ass off, took all the classes, read personal development books weekly, went on retreats... You name it, and I can tell you, I did it.

And a few years later, I now know why it didn't do a damn thing towards me being wealthy.

Working harder is NOT the answer to having wealth.

"But Sarah, so and so says..."

No, my dear, they are wrong.

Hard work can be part of creating wealth, but it is not the answer to having, keeping, attracting, and sustaining wealth, and in most cases, hard work is the exception, but not the rule.

The rule is -> you get to be wealthy because you decide you deserve it.

END OF STORY.

Maybe you picked up this book because you know me, or perhaps you are brand new to me. If you do not know me yet, I am the founder of The Savvy Networker Global, now open in 36 cities, supporting business owners from every walk of life who are in various stages of their journey; some, with the worst money mindset I have ever experienced. It is no wonder I felt compelled to write this book.

You see, alongside running a global company, I also work with bad-ass coaches who are ready to be the authority figure in their industry. What does this mean? They have to freakin' LOVE making money because achieving success with authority marketing means money flows in with ease, and almost always in higher amounts, more frequently.

I thought to myself, this can't be the best-kept secret for my high ticket clients, so I started to spread the message of money mindset to all 15,000 entrepreneurs I work with. Result... I'll let you know how it goes in a later book. For now, what I can say is, everyone who's taken my course has shown major growth in their business and personal wealth. How far they will take it, you will have to wait and see.

Over the next 30 days, you are going to learn how to treat money so that you can get it, use it, replenish it, and keep it.

Here is the phrase I want you to start using every time you let go of even a single penny: *There is always more where that came from!*

This will be the reminder you need that you are a friggin'

bad-ass wealthy babe and money flows into you like those cupcakes you tried to avoid eating last week.

Don't worry girl, I was right there with you!

The thing is, money is all around you, and as long as you treat it right, it will continue to be yours in amounts far greater than you have ever imagined.

If you are feeling broke as fuck right now, it's because you have a bad relationship with money and we'll get to that a little later on in the book. For now, it's time to start adopting a healthy money mindset.

You deserve to be wealthy as fuck!

You deserve to feel good about money.

You deserve to have all the money you can imagine and more.

You deserve to spend money on whatever you like without feeling guilty.

You deserve to be debt-free.

You deserve to be financially secure.

And now, my beautiful new friend, let's get you there.

The thing you need to understand about money is that you get to decide the level you play at.

You want to be rich, wealthy, and healthy? Then you need to climb your ass up there, stand tall, and live that sexy-ass life you want.

Yep, you heard me. Each time you want to claim something: Wealth, health, career, location, whatever it is you dream of, climb your ass up there and just decide it's where you belong. No one can take it away from you but you. You ultimately get to decide what you deserve in this life, so if you've been short on wishes come true, it's time to dive into what you believe you deserve because let me tell you, YOU DESERVE IT ALL, and then some.

This book was developed as a support tool to *100 Journal Prompts for Ready to Be 6 and 7 Figure coaches* (applicable even if you're a business owner of any sort).

What I have come to learn over the years is that money comes easily to me ALWAYS. And it's not because I work 24/7 or because I give up things to have it, but because I know without a doubt it's coming. I always trust this, and the world delivers.

This is the same thing I want for you, to live in the truth, that money is easy to have and the world will always give you more than what you need, as long as you ask for it and believe in it.

The next 30 days are all about taking your existing mindset and tossing it out the window. I like to call it *quantum leaping success*—going from where you are to a dramatic shift into something new and different, something better than you imagined.

Before you ask yourself what the secret is to achieve this, I will tell you. It's so simple you may want to chuck this book out the window, but don't, because that very same thought process IS what is holding you back. You believe it has to be hard, and, well, it doesn't.

I'm not just saying think it into existence. I'm saying you can just decide to be wealthy, have it all, make the most out of this life you've been given. Sure, you may have to get your hands dirty some days, but it would be boring if you didn't have to.

You may even have to call that creditor you've been ignoring or fill out that paperwork that's hiding in the bottom of your drawer but, this is part of having it all, doing the work AND trusting FULLY that the world will give you EVERYTHING you need.

So let's get to work, you gorgeous wealthy woman. Wealth is all around you and we are going to use the next 30 days together to bring it into existence.

I suggest grabbing a journal and journaling each day. Even if it's a one-liner, just jot down a wealth statement. I've added a few in the back of the book to get you going.

Get Your Copy Here
https://www.amazon.com/dp/B098TY1J7M

A SNEAK PEEK INSIDE
100-DAY JOURNAL
PROMPTS FOR READY TO
BE 6 & 7 FIGURE
COACHES

Rolling out of bed, I stretched my arms up high into the sky. My flowy white pyjama pants and gold sparkle PJ top wrapped around me. I looked out the window and thought to myself, *"Holy shit, this is everything I ever dreamed of. I fucking did it, and didn't I prove all the haters wrong!"* My bare feet felt so good on the floor as I walked over to brush my teeth and then onto the yoga mat. My yoga room soaked in the smell of tangerine and mint with the sun beaming in, it was spectacular. Again I thought to myself, *"Wow, I've created an amazing life."*

As I left the yoga mat, sipping a hot cup of matcha, I reached for my journal and my favourite gold colour pen. And there it was, a moment that took place every single day like my own personal religion. The moment that was sacred: never to be interrupted, never to be ignored, and most importantly, never to be rushed. It was time to journal.

Words would pour out of me daily that sometimes felt

like they made ZERO sense. Heck, I am sure most of it did make no sense, but the things that DID make sense, holy shit, those things were like magic.

When my pen hit the paper everything became real. It's always been like connecting to my soul or my higher power if you will.

My journal was the one place I knew I could be completely raw, without fear, always. I could be anything I wanted on those pages and at the same time, I could be everything I didn't want to be because no one was reading but me.

I dreamed BIG.
I let myself get wild and crazy.
I let myself get downright angry.
I worked out my frustration.
I strategized my business.
I even dreamed about love.

My journaling wasn't just about writing though. After each and every session, it is a sacred practice to close my eyes and visualize what I had created on those pages, what I wanted to let go of in life, and what I desired. And day after day, I noticed that these things began to come into my life with ease, like actual flipping ease. Do you even know how incredible that feeling is?

Since I am always about sharing my truths, I had no friggin' clue what ease felt like. In fact, at first, it was so foreign to me, it felt REALLY uncomfortable. I was always waiting for the other shoe to drop, and so I began journaling about what life would look like if the shoe didn't drop and if my life just kept moving forward in the most amazing ways.

And that's exactly what happened. It moved forward, and it was fucking amazing. Wait, it IS fucking amazing.

I encourage you to create your own journaling ritual. Think of it as a recipe. What do you need to make it good?

Candles?
Natural light?
Complete quiet?
Music?
Essential Oils?
A special space in your home?

Whatever it may be, make it yours and make sure it feels good for you. Journaling is just as much about the process as it is the outcome.

You will see what I mean as you continue through the next 100 days.

HOW THIS WORKS

I ask you a question or make a prompt and you go and answer it, in written form, in your journal.

Sounds pretty simple, doesn't it?

Here's the thing, if any question makes you feel like you do NOT want to answer it, I'd be seriously looking at the WHY to this. Because it's a sure sign you really need to do some work.

I really want you to watch out for questions that trigger you or make you feel massive resistance towards them. Investigating these ones with depth will help you have the most transformation, in my opinion.

Get Your Copy Here
https://www.amazon.com/dp/B092XGWVYF

ABOUT THE AUTHOR

Photo Credit: Vincent Turcot

Sarah Quinn is an entrepreneur and writer, real estate investor, and officially has her own clothing line. Sarah is based in Quebec City. When she isn't furiously unleashing her true message via Facebook Lives or her podcast, A Poor Coaches Guide to A Rich Life https://anchor.fm/apoorcoachesguide, she is running her online coaching business as an entertainer, speaker and success mentor to coaches around the globe.

With a new series of books, over a decade in online business, and several hundred product and event launches under her belt, Sarah is known as a Content Queen who just doesn't stop. She believes that you CAN have it all, on your terms, so long as you're willing to get honest with yourself about what you're really here to do in the world, and her mission in life is to help coaches learn to use their voice and day to day life as a powerful tool to inspire themselves and others to lead with authenticity, creating a life wilder than their wildest dreams.

Sarah is also a mom of 2 and is obsessed with teaching her children that you can have it all, exactly as you want and on your terms.

Sarah is also an expert in "No B.S" coaching and would love to help you create a business you love, completely on your terms!

Follow Sarah here:
Facebook:
https://www.facebook.com/coachesmakingmoney

OTHER BOOKS BY SARAH QUINN

Quit Fucking Around Series:

Have It All: 30-Day Money Mindset for Coaches: Step-Up, Let
Money and Success Flow

https://www.amazon.com/dp/Bo98TYiJ7M

Coded For Money, Flow and Fame: The Difference Between You
Chasing Clients Them And Chasing You

https://www.amazon.com/dp/Bo9FQC5PF3

It's All Fucking Possible: Your Guide to Overcoming an 'Impossible'
Goal.

https://www.amazon.com/dp/Bo98TYiJ7M

SO WHAT NOW?

As a special thank you for reading my book, I'd welcome you into my kick-ass Facebook Group- Coded For Money, Flow and Fame.

Join and Introduce Yourself right here:
CODED FOR MONEY, FLOW AND FAME
https://www.facebook.com/groups/688395964913660

ABOUT RED THREAD PUBLISHING

ABOUT

Red Thread

Connect

redthreadbooks.com
info@redthreadbooks.com

Stories Change Lives

We believe in the power of women's voices & stories to change the world. We support women not only to write & publish their books but to really embrace their voice, accelerate empowerment & reach global impact. Because women matter.

Do you have a story that must be told?

Sierra Melcher, author & founder of @RedThreadPublishing, & our team will support you every step of the way. Redthreadbooks.com

LEAVE A REVIEW

If you have enjoyed or found value from this book, please take a moment to leave an honest/brief review on Amazon https://www.amazon.com/dp/B09FQC5PF3. Your reviews help prospective readers decide if this is right for them & it is the greatest kindness you can offer the author.

Thank you in advance.

Made in the USA
Middletown, DE
12 January 2022

58513862R00052